YOUR FAITH / YOUR COMMITMENT / GOD'S CALL

confirm
PARENT GUIDE

APPROVED UNITED METHODIST CONFIRMATION

Confirm Parent Guide
Your Faith. Your Commitment. God's Call.

Copyright © by 2016 Cokesbury

CONFIRM is an official resource for The United Methodist Church, approved by Discipleship Ministries (General Board of Discipleship) and published by Youth Ministry Partners and Cokesbury, The United Methodist Publishing House, 2222 Rosa L. Parks Blvd., PO Box 280988, Nashville, TN 37228-0988.

No part of this work may be reproduced or transmitted in any form or by any means, electronic or mechanical, including photocopying and recording, or by any information storage or retrieval system, except as may be expressly permitted by the 1976 Copyright Act or in writing by the publisher.

Requests for permission should be addressed to Permissions Office, 2222 Rosa L. Parks Blvd., PO Box 280988, Nashville, TN 37228-0988. You may fax your request to 615-749-6128.

Scripture quotations unless noted otherwise are from the Common English Bible. Copyright © 2011 by the Common English Bible. All rights reserved. Used by permission. www.CommonEnglishBible.com

To order copies of this publication, call toll-free 800-672-1789. You may fax your order to 800-445-8189. Telecommunication Device for the Deaf-Telex Telephone: 800-227-4091. Or order online at cokesbury.com. Use your Cokesbury account, American Express, Visa, Discover, or MasterCard.

The Cross and Flame is a registered trademark and the use is supervised by the General Council on Finance and Administration of The United Methodist Church. Permission to use the Cross and Flame must be obtained from the General Council on Finance and Administration of The United Methodist Church: Legal Department, GCFA, PO Box 340029 Nashville, TN 37203-0029; Phone: 615-369-2334; Fax: 866-246-2516.

Writer: Wendy Mohler-Seib

16 17 18 19 20 21 22 23 24 25 — 10 9 8 7 6 5 4 3 2 1

MANUFACTURED IN THE UNITED STATES OF AMERICA

Contents

Introduction 5
Chapter 1: Why Confirm? 10
Chapter 2: Hitting the Mark 25
Chapter 3: You Matter Most 37
Chapter 4: Activities for Home 58

Meet the Writer

Rev. Wendy Mohler-Seib is the Director of Faith Formation for Youth and Young Adults at The Institute for Discipleship. Wendy is an ordained elder in the Great Plains Annual Conference of The United Methodist Church. She is a 2001 graduate of Southwestern College, with a B.A. in Religion and Philosophy, and a 2012 graduate of Princeton Theological Seminary, with an M.A. and an M.Div. Her studies focused in the area of youth ministry. Wendy has served in youth ministry in churches in Kansas, Florida, and New Jersey. She has also served as an associate pastor and senior pastor in Wichita, Kansas. Wendy loves preaching, teaching, and engaging in theological discussions.

Introduction

Give a youth worker a room full of 500 teenagers, and the youth worker knows exactly what to do. Youth workers love teenagers; they love talking about faith. They especially love talking with teenagers about their faith! However, when it comes to talking to the teenager living under our roof, it can be as awkward as the fifth-grade puberty presentation.

Youth workers pray with overwhelmed parents, tie stinky shoes to the top of the church van, climb the 35-foot pole on the high ropes course at camp every year, and consider all of the ways to impart faith into the lives of teenagers.

Youth workers know the heartache of teens walking away from the Christian faith, floundering in poor decision-making, or even committing suicide. They have rejoiced with young people living into God's calling. They've celebrated when teens let God transform their lives and began to use their gifts to transform the world. Certainly, they've learned the sufficiency of God's grace in human weakness, and God's trustworthiness with the teens they love and serve. Through ministry, youth workers discover the faithfulness of a God who never stops pursuing us.

PARENT PRACTICE
Reflect on the priorities you want for your teenager's faith. What are you doing to give priority to your teen's relationship with God?

Through research and hands-on experience, youth workers, like parents, know the most important lesson—there is always more to learn when it comes to teenagers and faith. Experiencing youth ministry from the parental angle is infinitely more terrifying! As parents, all our fears would be eradicated and such pressure relieved if we could get our hands on a foolproof plan for raising highly committed Christian young people. We are here because God has blessed us with children, and we want to come alongside our pastors, youth workers, and teenagers through this sacred educational and spiritual journey of confirmation.

Explicit and Implicit Curriculum

Education always includes *explicit* and *implicit* curriculum. In school, the explicit curriculum is the formal instruction—what's in the textbook or plan. In parenting, the explicit curriculum is the information you intentionally teach your children. This includes simple practices such as teaching your children to brush their teeth. Explicit curriculum teaches your child from an early age how to share, show kindness, and use words like *please* and *thank you*.

PARENT PRACTICE
Take a few moments to make a list of the explicit lessons that you have prioritized in your home.

The implicit, or accidental, curriculum refers to the hidden curriculum or the unwritten, unintentional lesson. In school, an example of hidden curriculum is the development of a positive attitude toward mathematics. At home, implicit curriculum also educates children based on what is behind the scenes. This includes observation and experience over direct instruction, such as when you put your cell phone away while driving, gathering at the dinner table, or going through the line at the grocery store. The implicit curriculum teaches your teenager that you value the lives of others on the road, that you care about your relationships with your family, and that greeting the cashier is more important than playing Candy Crush.

If you examine the explicit and implicit curriculum around the topic of God, what do your teenagers learn from you? Who explicitly teaches your teens about God, the Bible, and the church? How did they learn about Christ for the first time? Who is helping them put words to their encounters with God? What sayings, phrases, or ideas are being explicitly taught to them about God? What are your teenagers implicitly learning about God through the church or others? What do you wish you would have known about God in your adolescence, and how are you conveying this to your teenagers?

PARENT PRACTICE
Reflect on your own faith journey. Who taught you the faith? Write a letter to thank someone who has been instrumental in your own faith formation. Make a list of the people who have been influential—throughout your life—in helping you to recognize God's presence in your life. Journal about the attributes of God that are most important to you, and remember who taught you these truths about God.

Faith curriculum matters. Imagine your teen explicitly hearing again and again from a church community, "God is with you. God never abandons you." Now, imagine your teen facing a deep, dark depression. How is the explicit curriculum reinforced when the adult volunteers in the youth ministry rally around your teen and offer encouragement, support, and unconditional love in the wake of depression? How is the explicit curriculum undone if no one notices that the once exuberant and active young person is no longer present in worship, Bible study, or service projects? In a perfect world, the church's explicit and implicit curriculum match. In a perfect parenting scenario, our explicit and implicit curriculum about God match, too. Thank God that in our imperfect world the Holy Spirit fills in any gaps!

In the best-case scenario, pastors, parents, and youth workers ensure that the explicit curriculum and implicit curriculum about God's character match. This creates fertile ground for God to work. This requires teachers to be intentional, and it invites pastors, parents, and youth workers to actively consider how we teach the Christian faith.

Stop for a moment of reflection. How did the Christian faith become real to you? Who taught you the faith? Think about the inconsistencies you wrestled with in the implicit and explicit curriculum you experienced in your teenage years. Now consider the implicit and explicit teachings you're sharing with your teen regarding her faith. If you're really brave, ask your teenager to tell you what they've learned about God from you.

PARENT PRACTICE
While taking a drive with your teen this week, share your story. Tell how God became real to you. Be vulnerable and share the questions or musings you still have about God.

What to Expect

This family guide is not "how to do confirmation right." In fact, one right way doesn't exist—but many right ways do. Unfortunately, this guide can't guarantee your teenager has a great confirmation experience. Nor does it suggest that developing your teen's faith is easy. It's hard! Hopefully, this guide raises awareness for you to engage in conversations and activities with your teenager throughout confirmation, while also receiving clarity about the confirmation process in order to be an educated and encouraging parent throughout this process.

PARENT PRACTICE
On a scale of 1–10, rank your knowledge and understanding of the confirmation process. To know more, e-mail your teen's confirmation class leader, asking the leader to highlight the leader's priorities for confirmation.

The guide provides research-based facts, convictions, and action items to foster a deeper relationship with your teenager around matters of faith. It also offers a number of "Parent Practice" insets throughout the guide that encourage you to think about your role in your teen's confirmation and faith formation as well as to deepen your own relationship with Christ and the church. The No. 1 goal of the guide is to empower you to increase the Christian faith conversations in your home, specifically regarding confirmation.

Your family may pray before every meal, serve weekly in the soup kitchen, and read daily devotions every evening. Conversely, you may argue on the way to church, when you occasionally attend, and hardly talk at all—much less about your faith. Wherever you fall on the spectrum, and with whatever knowledge you and your teen bring to confirmation, this guide will encourage you, give you food for thought, and serve as a resource for thoughtful conversations about faith.

May we grow in our love for God and others through this experience. May our confidence in educating our young people in the faith grow, too. Let's get started!

1 Why Confirm?

Confirmation: A Continuum of Baptism

If you had your child baptized as an infant, you may remember getting everything in order before the baptism: inviting people, lining up a photographer, and dry cleaning your great-grandmother's baptismal gown for your child to wear. Do you remember the emotion welling up inside of you as you handed your child to the pastor? How about that moment when your voice was joined by the voices of an entire congregation as you took vows to raise your child together to trust Jesus? At the heart of United Methodist baptism is grace—grace for the child, parents, and entire faith community.

At your child's baptism, we recognized God's grace at work in your child, you promised to raise your child in the way that leads to life everlasting, and the faith community agreed to stand beside you and your child in faith development.

Confirmation is a continuation of what God started in baptism; for that matter, confirmation is a continuation of what God started in the community of faith in your child's baptism. While confirmation is the moment your teenager confirms the vows taken on his or her behalf in the baptism, it remains a communal experience, whereby the church sees the faithfulness of God at work in and through your teenager. At confirmation, your teen publicly professes personal faith in Christ and commits to faithful stewardship of time, talent, treasure, witness, and service in the body of Christ and the world. In baptism, we are initiated into the family of God, and in confirmation we publicly declare our allegiance to Christ and Christ's church.

Some parents reading this did not have their children baptized as infants. That's OK! Baptism is still a part of the confirmation continuum. If teenagers have not been baptized, they will have that opportunity before being confirmed in the church. If young people elect to be baptized and confirmed, they will take the baptismal vows for themselves, instead of parents taking vows on their behalf.

Let's look over the baptismal vows from The Baptismal Covenant I from *The United Methodist Book of Worship*.

The pastor addresses parents or other sponsors and those candidates who can answer for themselves:

On behalf of the whole Church, I ask you:
Do you renounce the spiritual forces of wickedness,
    reject the evil powers of this world,
    and repent of your sin?

I do.

Do you accept the freedom and power God gives you
    to resist evil, injustice, and oppression
    in whatever forms they present themselves?

I do.

Do you confess Jesus Christ as your Savior,
put your whole trust in his grace,
and promise to serve him as your Lord,
in union with the Church which Christ has opened
    to people of all ages, nations, and races?

I do.

The pastor addresses parents or other sponsors of candidates not able to answer for themselves:

Will you nurture these children (persons)
in Christ's holy Church,
that by your teaching and example they may be guided
    to accept God's grace for themselves,

to profess their faith openly,
and to lead a Christian life?

I will.

The pastor addresses candidates who can answer for themselves:

According to the grace given to you,
will you remain faithful members of Christ's holy Church
and serve as Christ's representatives in the world?

I will.

The pastor addresses the sponsors:

Will you who sponsor these candidates
support and encourage them in their Christian life?

I will.

The pastor addresses the congregation, and the congregation responds:

Do you, as Christ's body, the Church,
reaffirm both your rejection of sin
    and your commitment to Christ?

We do.

Will you nurture one another in the Christian faith and life
and include these persons now before you in your care?

With God's help we will proclaim the good news
    and live according to the example of Christ.
We will surround these persons
    with a community of love and forgiveness,
    that they may grow in their trust of God,
    and be found faithful in their service to others.
We will pray for them,
    that they may be true disciples
    who walk in the way that leads to life....

A deacon or pastor addresses all, and the congregation joins the candidates and their parents and sponsors in responding:

Let us join together in professing the Christian faith
    as contained in the Scriptures of the Old and
    New Testaments.
Do you believe in God the Father?

I believe in God, the Father Almighty,
    creator of heaven and earth.

Do you believe in Jesus Christ?

I believe in Jesus Christ, his only Son, our Lord,
    [who was conceived by the Holy Spirit,
    born of the Virgin Mary,
    suffered under Pontius Pilate,
    was crucified, died, and was buried;
    he descended to the dead.
    On the third day he rose again;
    he ascended into heaven,
    is seated at the right hand of the Father,
    and will come again to judge the living and the dead.]

Do you believe in the Holy Spirit?

I believe in the Holy Spirit,
    [the holy catholic church,
    the communion of saints,
    the forgiveness of sins,
    the resurrection of the body,
    and the life everlasting.][1]

Copyright © 1992, 2009 by The United Methodist Publishing House. Used by permission. All rights reserved.

John Wesley described baptism as a means of grace, which is unconditional love. Baptism is a conduit for God's grace to be poured out on a person—it is God's unfailing act of love, which is not dependent upon our response to God. As one of only two sacraments in The United Methodist Church, baptism is an outward sign of an inward grace or an inward working of God in human life. Baptism is not magical; God is not performing magic on the baptized. However, God is doing something extraordinary in the life of the baptized. God is marking the children in baptism and initiating the baptized into the family of God. Very simply stated, baptism is an outward sign that you and I belong to Christ, and this grace is based on God's love, not our response.

Confirmation is a time of owning for one's self the responsibility of surrendering one's life to God. If you didn't have your child baptized as an infant, this is when your teen is baptized and receives the extraordinary grace of God given in baptism and is initiated into Christ's family, and when the vows are declared by your teen as an affirmation of faith in both his or her baptism and confirmation. Each young person is confirming God's work in his or her life and the desire to commit to following Christ. Consider baptism and confirmation as major mile markers along a lifetime Christian journey.

PARENT PRACTICE
Review the baptismal and confirmation vows, and consider your own Christian faith. How are you living out these vows? How could you reorganize your time to fulfill your vows more faithfully?

Unfortunately, young people often engage in the confirmation class or experience only to "graduate church" after confirmation. This means they treat it like high school graduation—they walk across the "stage" and never come back. Pastors and youth workers wish this weren't the case! Through confirmation, we encounter wonderful young people! We share deep theological conversations, and often see a hunger for God developing. But sadly, many—as soon as they stand before the congregation on Confirmation Sunday, looking so poised for their photographs—disappear from church. This heightens concerns about our approach to confirmation. More importantly, this supports the claim that you—the parent—play an enormous role in nurturing your children's faith, more than you might realize. Believe it or not, your teen is following your lead! If you deem confirmation as serious, they take it more seriously. If you deem the Christian life beyond confirmation as serious, they take the Christian life more seriously!

The experience of watching young people go through confirmation and then graduate church is one reason pastors and youth workers give teenagers permission to decide whether or not to be confirmed. We want teens to know that taking vows before God and the Christian community should not be taken lightly. Vows matter! Following Jesus is not like signing up for a 5K or for musical tryouts to see if that is one's thing. Adults must not push young people to take vows they are not ready to take. God repeatedly pursues us over time, and we repeatedly have opportunities to say yes to Christ's call.

In his book *The Continuing Conversion of the Church*, retired Princeton Theological Seminary Professor Dr. Darrell Guder says the church is continually experiencing conversion.[2] In other words, we find ourselves as individuals and communities repeatedly at the foot of the cross seeking forgiveness and renewal of our commitment—our "yes" to the invitation to follow Christ in God's mission. How would the church's thinking around confirmation change if we viewed confirmation as one opportunity of many for young people to say yes to Christ? Put another way, confirmation at its very best is one significant public yes in a long line of yeses in following Christ!

PARENT PRACTICE
Reflect on how you've talked with your teen about confirmation. How have you described the vows? Does your teen feel safe to say that she's not ready to take the confirmation vows? Does your teen know that he alone will decide whether to be confirmed or not, and that you will not decide on his behalf?

The true aim of confirmation is focused learning, soul-searching, and intentional faith formation. We then allow young people to decide whether or not they are

Why Confirm? 15

ready to respond to God by taking the public vows. Joy and freedom come when we give individuals the opportunity to profess their faith for themselves, while we also recognize this as one of many moments when Christ invites your teenager to say yes to Christian discipleship.

Propelled into Deeper Discipleship

True discipleship is a daily journey of answering Christ's call to "Come, follow me!" Every day, in every decision, situation, and interaction, you and I choose whether or not to follow Christ. Likewise, every day teenagers will make choices about following Jesus. Confirmation is one of many steps in a lifetime of faithful discipleship—of choosing to say yes to Jesus. It is an important first step whereby your teen may courageously learn from your faith and trust Jesus for himself or herself. Now Christianity becomes your teen's personal faith within the context of the larger faith community. The baptismal vows are no longer yours alone; they are your teen's vows.

PARENT PRACTICE
When did you own your faith for yourself? Tell your teen about a time in your life when God became more real to you. Ask God to give you the words you need to share this with your teenager. Then, take a deep breath and start the conversation!

A United Methodist Understanding of Grace

My experience as a pastor confirms the modern notion that people don't choose a church based on denomination. When asked why people are at their current church, most often we hear, "I like the sermons" or "The people are great!" or "I love the children's ministry!" I don't generally hear folks say, "I am United Methodist and I was looking for a church that upholds *The Book of Discipline*." While many people do not always set out to find a United Methodist congregation, still our United Methodist theology undergirds the practices of our churches. What we believe about God determines how we act, and our actions mirror our beliefs. During confirmation, your teen will be learning about the distinct United Methodist Church beliefs. One of the most important of those beliefs is about grace.

My friends from another denomination often say, "You Methodists think you've cornered the market on grace; you know, you're not the only people with a theology of grace!" My friends are right; grace is not confined to The United Methodist Church. God's grace is universal. However, John Wesley had a unique understanding of grace that has informed and shaped how faithful Christians have lived their faith for over two centuries.

The United Methodist theology of grace is one of the most defining aspects of our denomination. John Wesley understood God's grace in three ways; prevenient grace (grace that goes before), justifying grace (saving grace), and sanctifying grace (growing grace). Our theology of grace is more than semantics or a nuanced way to talk about God's unmerited favor; it is central to our Christian identity and shapes the manner in which we live our Christian faith. Wesley's preaching revolutionized England because he preached that God's grace is free to all people, and all means ALL! Contrary to many of Wesley's contemporaries, Wesley taught that God's grace was not reserved for a specific elect group of people. His belief that God does not exclude anyone from the opportunity to live in God's grace propelled him to share God's love with prisoners, those facing severe poverty, alcoholics, destitute children, the sick, and those on the furthest margins of society. Still today, this underlying conviction that God's love is readily available to all people drives the way we practice our faith as United Methodists.

Prevenient Grace

Prevenient grace is also known as "preventing grace," which prevents us from going through life without the opportunity

PARENT PRACTICE
Write down a working definition of *grace* and save it for later.

to experience God. This is the grace of God that goes before us (Pre-). Prevenient grace is God's work in our lives before we are even able to recognize God.

You might have a memory of a moment in life when you were going through a tough time, and a stranger extended kindness to you during your all-time low. You couldn't describe the comfort and love you felt, yet something about it prompted you to say a simple prayer. Maybe that simple act of kindness that served as a gateway to prayer gave you the courage to try a new church, and that new church graciously welcomed you and pointed you to God's hope amid your difficult days. These moments exemplify God's prevenient grace, the grace that goes before us and "stirs up within us a desire to know God and empowers us to respond to God's invitation to be in relationship with God."[3]

Think back to preparations you made before your little one arrived. Whether you're a biological parent, a stepparent, an adoptive parent, a foster parent, or a legal guardian, you prepared yourself for your child's arrival. You began to rearrange your life in anticipation of her or his arrival. You readied a room and began to plan for a secure financial future—all to express love for a child who didn't yet know the depth, length, or width of your love—but soon will.

PARENT PRACTICE
Sit down in a quiet place with a cup of coffee or other favorite drink. Think of a moment when you experienced God's prevenient grace, and take a sip of coffee, giving thanks to God for unconditional love. Repeat this until your coffee is gone.

In the same way, the prevenient grace of God is the grace that goes before you and me and prepares us to recognize God's love for us. Before God is recognizable to us, God goes before us and prepares the way for us to experience God.

In the United Methodist tradition, infant baptism is a mark of God's prevenient grace. Infants do not choose to receive this grace on their own. Your choice to raise your child in the way that leads to life eternal is prevenient grace in action. In infant baptism, God initiates the child into the family of God before a decision to follow Christ is possible. It is also a reminder to us that God always goes before us, always pursues us, and always precedes our own recognition of God's goodness.

Justifying Grace

Sin distorts the image of God in each one of us. The justifying grace of God restores us and reconciles us with God and one another. Justifying grace puts us in right relationship with Jesus Christ. "Through the work of God in Christ our sins are forgiven, and our relationship with God is restored."[4] When we experience the justifying grace of God, we undergo a conversion or a transformation. In this transformation, we reorient our lives around Christ by repenting from our sins and turning our hearts and minds away from sin and toward God. In this time of transformation, we find assurance as our spirit testifies with God's Spirit that we belong to Christ.[5]

PARENT PRACTICE
When did you respond to the justifying grace of God? Was it a specific moment of conversion, or did you say yes to Christ over a period of time? Practice sharing this part of your faith story by writing your story out or telling it to your partner or a close friend. Pray for the opportunity to share this story with a friend, a co-worker, or a family member or your teen.

The United Methodist Church does not teach that the decision to follow Christ always takes place at one specific moment in time. Maybe you've been asked by a Christian from another denomination, "When were you saved?" This type of language is rare for United Methodists, because we believe that God saved all people in the life, death, and resurrection of Christ. The one-time moment of

Why Confirm? 19

Christ's death on the cross, and resurrection three days later, defeated death for every person in all of history, once and for all. The saving moment is not the moment you or I decide to receive God's gift of salvation. The justifying grace of God is shown and realized in life when one responds to it in the choice to follow Jesus Christ as Savior and Lord.

For some Christians, the decision to follow Christ occurred in a decisive moment that completely reoriented their lives, so they say, "That's when I became a Christian." For others, the justifying grace of God is realized over time when yes was said to God's invitation to follow Christ in the midst of many encounters and situations.

Matt volunteered in the local high school's Fellowship of Christian Athletes and attended a United Methodist church in rural Kansas. In Sunday school, Matt said, "I don't know an exact moment when I became a Christian. I just remember a number of times I said yes to Jesus. I woke up one day and realized I was a Christian." Matt experienced the justifying grace of God gradually.

Chris, on the other hand, found herself angry and distant from God. Through a strange series of events, Chris responded to an invitation to attend worship at a new United Methodist church in town. She had a bitter taste in her mouth toward Christianity, especially United Methodists, but through the prevenient grace of God at work in her life, she found herself one Sunday slipping in late to a worship service. In one moment, God clearly spoke to Chris and filled her with an assurance that God's love is real and that God wanted to bless her with a full, abundant life free of condemnation and shame. In an instant, Chris's whole life was reoriented as she turned away from sin and toward God.

Confirmation is a time for teens to publicly affirm the recognition of God's saving grace and declare their intent to follow Christ and live in Christian community. In this affirmation, they confirm the grace poured out upon them in their baptism, and publicly acknowledge that they are putting their whole trust in Christ as their Savior and Lord. They are declaring their intent to orient their lives around Christ.

Sanctifying Grace

John Wesley identified the sanctifying grace of God as what moves us to perfection. Now, there's a word that can trip you up: *perfection*. This is one of the most distinctive theological concepts in The United Methodist Church. Wesley's understanding of Christian perfection (sanctifying grace) separated him from his contemporaries and still distinguishes Wesleyans from other Christian denominations today. Sanctification is an ongoing transformation. It is the process of becoming like Christ.

The idea that we grow in the image of Christ is sometimes hard to imagine, but through a relationship with Christ, God moves us toward maturity, completion, or wholeness. This gets tricky to talk about because we associate perfection with flawlessness. As babies mature, they go from sitting to crawling, then to preschool, kindergarten, elementary school, and middle school, and then on to college or a career; to grow and mature in our relationships with God and others also has a progression. Like babies who mature over time to be able to crawl and later to read and finally to present complex thoughts, we grow in our faith from immaturity to maturity as the fruit of the Spirit increases in our lives and as we dedicate more time and energy listening and obeying God's voice. As love increases in our lives, sin decreases and our inner and outer lives become more and more aligned with Christ.[6]

PARENT PRACTICE
Will you open yourself to God's movement as your teen encounters God? Consider one way that God is moving in your life. How might you respond to God's invitation?

Give Them Grace

What about the teenager in the confirmation class who is not yet ready to make a vow

Why Confirm? 21

to follow Jesus? Sometimes this causes parental feelings of consternation. Here's the reality: a number of young people go through confirmation because they think they're required to. Maybe you had a battle in your own home over confirmation, and your young person is going with heels dug into the ground. While his or her attitude may make you wonder if you've done the right thing, remember that God loves your teenager even more than you do!

It's so hard to trust God with this most valuable relationship. God's prevenient grace is going before your teen, and God has already demonstrated the ultimate love for your precious one in the life, death, and resurrection of Christ. Encourage your teen to complete confirmation, trust God's work, be gracious and supportive of her faith journey, and give space for the Holy Spirit—even if she doesn't grow at your desired pace.

One young person I had the privilege of having in confirmation wasn't ready to be confirmed. He finished all of the work of the class and then went to his parents to inform them of his decision not to be confirmed. Although this deeply pained his parents, they honored their son's request, and committed to prayer and open conversations about faith in their home. Before their son graduated from high school, he went to his parents and told them that he was ready to become a confirmed member of his local church. He was ready to own his parents' baptismal vows as his own. In time, he received and realized the justifying grace of God in a transformative way. Today, he is a devout follower of Christ.

This story reminds us of the prevenient grace of God and assures us that God constantly pursues every person. God's desire is for each person to experience and receive the justifying grace of God, and then to grow as God's sanctifying grace brings us to maturity in Christ. Yet God respects the readiness of each individual. It is important for parents to trust our children into God's care! Remember your adolescent years? Remember your own journey of faith and the difficulty even now to hear God's voice? This is meaningful, hard work! A relationship with God cannot be zapped in a microwave oven. Confirmation is one part of the journey, and we hope our teens will receive and acknowledge God's saving grace at the end of the process. Some teens may be reluctant to make such a significant commitment and will need your permission to wait and help as they continue to explore their faith.

The bottom line is that God's salvation comes to us through Christ. Your teen may be ready to confirm God's saving grace with her or his confirmation class, or may not for several years. We each experience God's grace and salvation at different times through different avenues. There is not a right way for teens to experience confirmation. For some, confirmation will be the first time they recognize God's saving grace; for others, this will be another pivotal moment they recognize God's saving grace and publicly make their confirmation vows; and for others, this will be a time to deeply consider the saving grace of God, but not the time to make a public affirmation of faith. Still for others, this will be a deeply sanctifying experience that jump-starts their spiritual transition from a young Christian into a maturing Christian.

No matter where your teen lands along that spectrum, consider confirmation a highway marker on a long road trip of faith. Confirmation is not the final destination on the journey; it is a significant mile marker and designated stop for teenagers to intentionally focus on growing in their relationship with God. It's a safe space for adolescents to consider their response to God's grace.

Chapter 1 Notes

1. From "The Baptismal Covenant I" in "The Services of the Baptismal Covenant of The United Methodist Church as Revised to Align with the 2008 Book of Discipline and Book of Resolutions," Copyright © 1989, 2009, The United Methodist Publishing House. Discipleship Ministries website, *tinyurl.com/j25ronf*. Accessed 2 August 2016. Churches have the option of omitting text within brackets.
2. Darrell L. Guder, *The Continuing Conversion of the Church* (Grand Rapids: William B. Eerdmans Publishing Co., 2000), page 150.
3. From "Our Wesleyan Heritage," The United Methodist Church website, *tinyurl.com/jhskrkx*. Accessed 1 August 2016.
4. From "Our Wesleyan Heritage."
5. From "Our Wesleyan Heritage."
6. From "Our Wesleyan Heritage."

2 Hitting the Mark

Ask a handful of golfers to identify the aim of golf, and you'll get a handful of responses. One may say, "To win with the lowest score." Another, "Exercise!" Yet another, "I enjoy the outdoors." Polling a handful of Christians on the aim of the Christian life could garner a variety of responses, too. Assuredly, many Christians would respond with Jesus' words to the Pharisees in Matthew 22:37-40:

> "*You must love the Lord your God with all your heart, with all your being,* and with all your mind. This is the first and greatest commandment. And the second is like it: *You must love your neighbor as you love yourself.* All the Law and the Prophets depend on these two commands."

The end goal is important. Confirmation points to the ultimate aim of the Christian life, which is to be made perfect (whole, complete, or mature) in our love for God and others. A clear mark keeps us from aimlessly wandering. The aim of the Christian life is maturity, and confirmation is a process that guides the movement of our young people toward the final goal. There may be times when your teenager bemoans attending confirmation, resists talking to you about class discussions, or becomes reluctant to stand before the church to take confirmation vows. Be encouraged by keeping the aim of the Christian life in perspective through this process. Pray that confirmation will strengthen your teen's relationship with Christ, serve as a rite of passage in the journey of faith, and shift the ownership of faith away from you and toward your teen. This is an important moment in your young person's life.

Parent Practice
Considering Matthew 22:37-40, how do Jesus' words increase your desire to foster faith in your teen? How do Jesus' words reduce your anxiety about teaching your teenager the Christian faith?

Burning Bushes and Blowing Trumpets

God is not afraid to coax us along. God gives us moments for growth in our faith journey and opportunities to respond to God's invitation. One of the most famous stories of call and response is the story of Moses and the burning bush in Exodus 3. A churchgoer asked, "How long do you think Moses stared at the bush before he realized it wasn't being consumed?" Now isn't that something to consider? Before God called Moses, God started a fire and kept it kindled long enough to catch Moses' attention. Once Moses stopped and noticed the bush was burning and not being consumed, Moses realized he was standing on holy ground. Then Moses engaged with God and responded to God's invitation to deliver the Israelites from slavery.

The burning bush was a watershed moment that led Moses to discover his purpose and call—to become Israel's deliverer. In times of doubt or insecurity, Moses could recall this burning bush experience and use it to regain confidence to accomplish God's mission. Moses could reflect on this event and be reminded of his identity, purpose, and faith. In this way, the burning bush experience provided fuel propelling him to complete God's mission to free the Israelites.

Then, there is Gideon's story in Judges 6–7. His tribe was the smallest of the Israelite tribes. God called Gideon to lead the Israelites against the Midianites in battle. God sent an angel, and when Gideon requested a sign that it was the Lord speaking to him, God sent a fire to burn up his meat and unleavened bread.

Later, Gideon wasn't quite convinced God intended to rescue Israel through Gideon, and decided he wanted proof. First, he put a dry fleece out to see if it would become wet with dew while the ground remained dry in the morning. Sure enough, the next morning, the fleece was dripping wet and the ground was dry. Gideon was still not convinced, so the next day he put the fleece out again, only this time asking God to make the ground wet and the fleece dry. In the morning, God answered Gideon's plea; the ground was wet and the fleece was dry, despite the dew.

To stretch Gideon's emerging trust, God trimmed Gideon's army from 32,000 men to 300, and to top it off, Gideon couragously led his small army into battle equipped with only trumpets and jars containing torches. After the Israelites smashed their jars, the torches in the jars created a bright light and the trumpets startled the enemy so badly that the terrified enemy camp began fighting among themselves. Gideon's army won without raising a sword.

Do you see the faithfulness of God for Gideon? In Gideon's willingness to say yes to God, God graciously gave Gideon pivotal and undeniable experiences along the way that served to develop Gideon's trust in God. These situations gave Gideon the faith and assurance he needed to answer God's calling and accomplish the aim of God's mission then and also in the future.

God's encounters with Moses and Gideon were both powerful and memorable. God invited them into a deeper faith, and, in both instances, required a response. God provided distinct moments for Moses and Gideon to own the shift God was making in their lives. God was moving them from community participants to community leaders. These experiences resulted in a transformation that was evident not just to them but also to others as well. God acted, Moses and Gideon responded, and others recognized the benefits of their willingness to be changed through these powerful encounters with God.

God is calling our teens as well. Confirmation is the result of God's grace and our response to God's activity. God is eager to transform our young people through confirmation. If we are open, our lives can be changed as well. We can experience God moving in and through our young people during this pivotal part of their faith development. Now, what will it take for confirmation to be as memorable as a burning bush or a blowing trumpet?

Confirmation, a Rite of Passage

By now, hopefully, we agree that God is active and working to pursue a meaningful relationship with our teens at every turn! We trust confirmation to be another place where God meets young people with another invitation to say yes to God and where they join God's mission in the world to serve others. When the church—empowered by the Holy Spirit—values, resources, and positions confirmation as a pivotal time in a young person's holistic development, the result is a clear pathway or rite of passage toward maturing spiritual adulthood.

PARENT PRACTICE
Looking back, do you recall any specific moments to signify the shifts in your faith journey? If you have no significant memories, what do you wish you had experienced? Look ahead to the last chapter of the book. Pick one activity to do with your teen.

A little over a century ago, the path to adulthood was clearer and children transitioned into adults at a much earlier age. In general, children moved from school into an apprenticeship followed by a job. Additionally, this meant they lived at home with their families until marriage. This has changed as the result of socioeconomic forces such as the industrial revolution that contributed to the emergence of adolescence as a developmental stage between childhood and adulthood. While confirmation is not intended to prepare young people to be fully functioning adults, it does serve as a time of preparation for adulthood and a rite of passage that promotes trusting in God and accepting new freedoms and responsibilities as full participants in the life of the congregation.

A rite of passage marks movement from childhood to adulthood. Rites of passage signify a shift for the individual and community. Jewish teenagers celebrate Bar Mitzvahs and Bat Mitzvahs. Hispanic girls celebrate Quinceaneras. Amish youth have Rumspringa, and many tribal cultures offer children distinct passageways into adulthood. What rites of passage can you think of that we offer teenagers, specific to the Christian faith? Without confirmation, we are hard pressed to offer one specific moment that ritualizes the maturation of their faith.

In general, rites of passage are associated with life cycles, crises, or important calendar dates.[1] When the rite of passage is associated with a life cycle observance, the transition moves a person from a dependent and defined role in the community to a new interdependent and empowered role. The rite of passage serves as a clear indicator of one's transformation[2] in the same manner that the first day of kindergarten, middle school, or high school indicates a distinct transition in the academic growth of our children.

Each rite of passage possesses three stages: separation, transition, and incorporation.[3] Separation signifies departing from a role such as when a person today leaves her role as a child to move toward becoming an adolescent. Transition is a space of limbo, called liminality, between the two roles, and incorporation recognizes arrival in the new role. If applied to confirmation, leaving children's ministry may signify the departure from childhood. Transition may be the period of confirmation. In this space, young people are not recognized as children in the congregation, nor are they seen as full members or guardians of their own faith. It is truly a space between roles. Finally, incorporation shifts the thinking of the young people and the congregation. Now, the confirmands are seen as full members of the congregation, and the confirmands identify their faith as their own. Incorporation means full participation and the same responsibilities and ownership as the adults in the congregation. What kind of energy is infused into a congregation when teenagers take as much ownership in the life of the church as the adults?

PARENT PRACTICE
Think about the ways your teen has developed over the years. How has he or she ...
- Physically grown and changed?
- Matured in gifts, passions, and skills?
- Changed or stayed the same in personality?

Compare the faith development and the physical development of your child. How would you categorize your teen's spiritual maturation?

For instance, at Kingston United Methodist Church in Kingston, New Jersey, integrating young people into the life and ministry of the congregation is foundational to who they are. The incorporation of confirmed members at KUMC is so central to the DNA of the congregation that Shannon never found it confusing or surprising when she was asked to preach when the pastor wanted a different voice in the pulpit. No one balked at fifteen-year-old Ian as he gave directions for the annual Christmas pageant he wrote. Conor didn't think twice about who would shovel the snow off of the driveway on any given Sunday in January, and Meghan never waited for an adult to ask her to help hide the Easter eggs for the children following the Easter Sunday service. For KUMC, this is not tokenism. Young people at KUMC lead because they are members of Christ's church. They agreed to uphold the church with their time, talent, treasure, service, and witness, and the community views them as faithful members in light of these vows.

Confirmation invites the congregation to shift their view of the confirmand and to incorporate the young person into the life of the church. The call to the congregation is to provide the necessary space, guidance, and resources to ensure that confirmed young people are able to fulfill these vows, and to honor them as members of Christ's body. How the church responds will go a long way in determining whether young people embrace confirmation as a rite of passage and commit fully to the life and ministry of Christ's church. What if we as parents fail to honor this shift in the lives of our teens? What does that signal to the other adults in our congregation?

Our young people still need our guidance, encouragement, and prodding in their faith journey. Let's be honest, even Jesus needed others. Understanding confirmation as a rite of passage does not relieve us from nurturing the faith of our teens after they are confirmed. It does give us clear spiritual markers to identify the growth and development of their faith on this journey. What would it look like for you to explicitly and implicitly express to your teen the way you see them maturing during and after confirmation? How will you embrace and support them after confirmation as they move from one role in the community of faith to another?

Avoiding Graduation

Many youth workers lament high school graduation because of the notion that high schoolers not only graduate from high school but also graduate from church never to return again. One survey researched whether youths who attended church for at least one year of high school actually "dropped out" of church.[4] The research discovered that 70 percent of all Protestant teenagers surveyed stopped attending church sometime between seventeen and nineteen years of age.

The most disconcerting part of the research is the reason the youths left the church: "Our teenagers aren't primarily leaving because they have significant disagreements with their theological upbringing or out of some sense of rebellion. For the most part, they simply lose track of the church and stop seeing it as important to their life."[5]

Today, pastors and youth workers alike lament the end of confirmation because it has become the time many young people stop participating in the church. How can your church reverse this trend?

Here are three motivators to keep young people engaged:

    1. Relevant biblical teaching that guides a young person's daily decisions.

2. Parents who are committed to their marriage and to following Jesus.

3. Adults (other than the teen's parent) who significantly invest in their lives.[6]

The convergence of a meaningful rite of passage, positive parental influence, and a Spirit-infused church who nurtures young people has been shown to be the most effective way to influence teens to continue their journey of discipleship after confirmation ends.[7] How can you as a parent surround your teen with others who will significantly impact them personally and spiritually? Are there young people in your congregation whom you can positively influence by your presence in their lives?

Millie was a confirmation student perhaps like yours, full of energy and inquisitiveness. Each week she posed hard questions about faith, science, and the Bible. It quickly became apparent that Millie's intellectual interests were equally matched with a compassionate, generous heart. When Millie participated in her one-on-one meeting with the associate pastor (a New Testament scholar) at the end of confirmation, she probed and prodded as she weighed her decision to publicly profess her faith and join the church Following Confirmation Sunday, Millie made a point to participate in the youth group's Bible studies. She also started consistently serving in the children's ministry. Two years after her confirmation, she was hired as an assistant in the Wednesday evening children's ministry, and she served on the church's administrative council. Millie's confirmation spurred her to grow spiritually through Bible study and service. In Millie's senior year, she led her congregation and community to collect shoes for a nonprofit organization that delivers gently used shoes to people in poverty around the world. Her efforts, rooted in her faith, attracted the attention of national news stations and celebrities who helped her reach her goal of 25,000 shoes. Millie's congregation views her as a dedicated disciple, a strong Christian leader, and an engaged member of her congregation.

Millie was like most every other confirmation student. What was the difference for her? Her congregation educated her in important biblical concepts applicable to her daily life. Millie's parents, particularly her father, encouraged faithful Christian discipleship, and many adults surrounded Millie in her spiritual journey. This is a powerful testimony of a young person responding to empowerment and significance as a full participant in the life of the local church following confirmation.

As wonderful a story as this is, Millie is not an example for what every confirmand should be and do. Each young person will have his or her own response. The most important lesson from Millie's story this: confirmation is not a culminating moment resulting in graduation from church. Rather, confirmation ritualizes the transformative work of God in the life of a teenager as the teen changes from a fledging child to an empowered young person responsible for furthering God's mission in the world.

Given Your Context...

Rites of passage are contextual. They vary by ethnic groups, region, faith tradition, and beyond. What helps one congregation recognize confirmation as a rite of passage may not work for another congregation. Your congregation may practice confirmation with sixth-graders while another congregation has eighth-graders in confirmation. So, given your congregation's context, consider ways you will support your teens' confirmation. How might you celebrate your teens' decision to say yes to a lifetime of discipleship?

Imagine how your teenager will remember confirmation if your energy toward confirmation exceeds your energy toward grades, athletic accomplishments, a driver's license, and so forth. Although your teen may not recognize confirmation as a seismic shift as they are experiencing it, hopefully, in hindsight, confirmation will be a rite of passage that shifts their mentality in establishing ownership of their Christian faith.

PARENT PRACTICE
What kind of celebration is offered for your confirmand? What could you do to further engage the celebration? What would it look like for you, along with your teen, to set up an invitation list of the people your young person wants to invite to her or his confirmation? What might your family do to celebrate beyond what the church offers? Will you make as big of a deal of confirmation as the sixteenth birthday or high school graduation? Why? Why not?

What does it look like for your community of faith to profoundly engage in the rite of confirmation? Our prayer is that Confirmation Sunday is not one of the Sundays that many adults skip because it "involves the youth." If that is the case, will you help be the change teenagers need? Ensure that confirmation not only is an individual faith experience but also is valued in your church community—invite other adults to be present, tell others how valuable they are to the lives of the young people in your church, and be the biggest advocate your church has ever seen for the rite of confirmation.

The community of faith took vows at your child's baptism, and confirmation is the congregation's opportunity to recommit to their ongoing partnership with you to develop the faith of your teen. After confirmation, your teenager is now part of the community of faith for the next generation of baptized children. If the culture in your congregation does not celebrate teenagers, you can be a catalyst for change. It is in the best interest of your teenager, and it is in the best interest of the church, the community, and the world.

The aim of the Christian faith is forward movement and maturation in love of God and love of neighbor. John Wesley said:

> What is then the perfection of which man is capable while he dwells in a corruptible body? It is the complying with that kind command, "My son, give me thy heart." It is the "loving the Lord his God with

all his heart, and with all his soul, and with all his mind." This is the sum of Christian perfection: It is all comprised in that one word, Love. The first branch of it is the love of God: And as he that loves God loves his brother also, it is inseparably connected with the second: "Thou shalt love thy neighbour as thyself:" Thou shalt love every man as thy own soul, as Christ loved us. "On these two commandments hang all the law and the prophets:" These contain the whole of Christian perfection.[8]

We arrive at Christian perfection one step at a time. Confirmation is one distinctive, pivotal step in a lifetime journey of spiritual growth and development that leads to a mature love of God and neighbor. Confirmation is a rite of passage that gives you, your young person, and your congregation the opportunity to signify and celebrate your teen's progression in the life cycle of faith formation. We can create an experience they will remember throughout their lifetime. They can know we value and support their faith decision unconditionally. Let's put ourselves fully into their confirmation experience with the same intentionality we put into helping them with other major life choices.

Chapter 2 Notes

1. James L. Cox, "Introduction: Ritual, Rites of Passage and the Interaction Between Christian and Traditional Religions," in *Rites of Passage in Contemporary Africa: Interaction Between Christian and African Traditional Religions*, ed. James L. Cox (Cardiff: Cardiff Academic Press, 1998), page x.
2. Cox, "Introduction: Ritual, Rites of Passage," page xi.
3. Cox, "Introduction: Ritual, Rites of Passage," xi. Cox cites the life cycle rites of passage according to Charles R. Taber, "Life Cycle Rites," in *Abingdon Dictionary of Living Religions*, ed. Keith Crim (Nashville: Abingdon, 1981), page 426.
4. Ed Stetzer, "Dropouts and Disciples: How Many Students Are Really Leaving the Church?," 14 May 2014, *Christianity Today* website, tinyurl.com/owovk8u. Accessed 3 August 2016.
5. Stetzer, "Dropouts and Disciples."
6. Stetzer, "Dropouts and Disciples."
7. John Roberto, "Best Practices in Adolescent Faith Formation," *Lifelong Faith* (Fall/Winter, 2007), page 52, tinyurl.com/glha8zh. Accessed 12 August 2016.
8. John Wesley, Sermon 76, "On Perfection," Section 1, in *The Sermons of John Wesley*, ed. Thomas Jackson, Global Ministries of the United Methodist Church website, tinyurl.com/h4qtvy7. Accessed 3 August 2016.

3 You Matter Most

You matter most! It's hard to believe, isn't it? When we see how obsessed adolescents are with friends, we assume our parental voice is irrelevant. When every word we offer is met with an eye roll, it's hard to believe our opinion holds any weight. There are days when our own doubts and insecurities leave us wondering if the little baseball-card-loving homework-hater will ever choose to enter a meaningful relationship with Jesus Christ. We wonder, "Is my faith even attractive to this teenager?"

As a young single youth director, I watched intently as parents navigated the difficult landscape of their teenagers' years. Of the many observations, one stood out: there seemed to be a connection between parental expectations about faith for their teens and their teens' actual faith development. I didn't know it, but at the same time, a sociological study was taking place that confirmed many of my observations.

Jack and Teresa parented two teenage girls. Jack and Teresa were active in adult Sunday school, weekly worship, hospitality, and administrative teams in the church. They understood the mission of God in the world. Each year with great zeal, they organized the church's annual Christmas mission of providing hundreds of Christmas gifts to children around the world. Jack served on the van ministry picking up senior adults and those without transportation to attend weekly worship. He never missed cheering on the church league women's softball team. Children, youth, and adults elbowed one another in the potluck line for Teresa's signature pizza rolls and apple dip. Jack and Teresa lived a life of faithful discipleship publicly and privately. They thoughtfully engaged their faith through prayer and Bible study. They regularly engaged in conversations about faith with their girls. While some of Jack and Teresa's peers expected their teenagers to do what "normal teenagers do," by rebelling in their youth and returning to their faith later in life, these parents thought differently. Jack and Teresa filled the minds and hearts of their girls with God-sized possibilities. With their lives and their words they taught the girls that a life following after Christ is full of opportunity, joy, and hope! Jack and Teresa believed that the faith of their children hinged on their own faith. They knew God entrusted them with teaching the faith to the best of their ability to their girls. Jack and Teresa demonstrated what has since been identified as foundational to a lasting faith: parental influence.

The Research Says

The National Study of Youth and Religion (NSYR) is the most extensive study of teenagers and faith formation conducted in the United States. The research from the NSYR explores the strengths and weaknesses of parents and churches. The NSYR concluded that parental faith matters in the life of your child! While exceptions always exist, "parents for whom religious faith is quite important are ... likely to be raising teenagers for whom faith is quite important, while parents whose faith is not important are likely to be raising teenagers for whom faith is also not important."[1] The fact that you've taken time to read this study guide means that you give thought to your child's faith.

The NSYR gives us significant insight about the influence that a parent has in the faith formation of teens. Here is a summary of what was learned about the role of parents in faith formation:

- The level of importance you place on your faith will likely be mirrored by your youth.[2]

- Parents play the most significant role in shaping the spiritual lives of teenagers.[3]

- "Teens who say their parents do not understand, love, or pay attention to them are more likely to be nonreligious than teens who say their parents do understand, love, and pay attention to them."[4]

- The vast majority of teenagers interviewed in the NSYR said their faith beliefs were what they were "raised to believe."[5]

- While other adults influence the faith of teenagers, the most important adult relationships to the faith of teenagers is the influence of a parent.[6]

Not only did the NSYR highlight our role as parents in the faith of our children, but the NSYR also revealed a multitude of other discoveries about teens and their faith. These findings can be used to guide our young people toward a lifetime of committed discipleship to Christ and provide us tools for examining our own faith. Here's what was learned:

- "Religion is a significant presence in the lives of many U.S. teens today."[7]

- Although teens are "impressively articulate" regarding many topics, U.S. teenagers are not able to discuss matters of faith very well. Sociologist Christian Smith believes the reason for this is that "no one has taught them how to talk about their faith."[8]

- Teenagers are content to receive the faith that has been handed to them, and they rarely spend time on personal spiritual quests.[9]

- "Religious congregations that prioritize ministry to youth and support for their parents, invest in trained and skilled youth group leaders, and make serious efforts to engage and teach adolescents seem much more likely to draw youth into their religious lives and to foster religious and spiritual maturity in their young members."[10]

- The most prominent faith of teenagers today is "Moralistic Therapeutic Deism" (MTD). Most teenagers in America think that faith is about being nice, feeling good, and recognizing God as a cosmic force out there, who is not necessarily involved in the daily lives of people.[11]

What does this research mean for us as parents? First, teens consider religion important, so as parents let's not downplay the role of God, church, Bible study, youth ministry, and other opportunities for our teens to grow in their faith. Next, teenagers are not naturally articulate and inquisitive about their faith — we teach them to be articulate and inquisitive. We can give them faith language and model a life that seeks God's wisdom and will, while placing them in a church culture that nurtures spiritual growth. It is important that our churches support young people. We want to be proactive in partnering with our local churches to foster our young people's spirituality. Finally, Moralistic Therapeutic Deism is not the religion of Jesus Christ. God is working all around us. God is on the move, and God desires to be involved in our daily lives. Following Christ cannot be reduced to "being nice" and "feeling good." A daily relationship with Christ calls us into sacrificial discipleship with a living, active, on-the-move God interested in partnering with us in every step of life's journey. Christianity is not passive. To offer our teenagers more than Moralistic Therapeutic Deism requires us to live in step with Christ, and practice our faith in word and deed.

Research is simultaneously both helpful and limited. It is helpful in offering insight, which, when applied to understanding, provides us wisdom in parenting. Yet, as helpful as research is in providing understanding of the adolescent landscape, it isn't the last word nor does it provide a foolproof formula for raising highly committed Christians. This is where trust in God's Spirit to work beyond what research concludes is critical. So using the tool of research and putting our trust in the God who loves them more than we ever can, here are three suggestions: Set aside time and energy for Christian education. Start talking. Make room for holy interruptions.

Let's Prioritize, Prioritize, Prioritize

"K-S-U WILDCATS! K...S...U...WILDCATS!"

In an instant, the wedding reception turned from vibrant dance floor into Kansas State University rally. Twenty-plus college students gathered around a young boy chanting the KSU cheer. He captured his audience! While he was one of the smallest bodies on the dance floor, he was not shy! He was full of energy, and every eye watched as adults followed his lead. This boy's family had indoctrinated him in KSU's culture well. He did not need guidance to mimic the movements, tones, and chants of KSU's mascot, Willy the Wildcat.

My niece's wedding dance-turned-rally reminded me of a recurring conversation with youth ministry friends in seminary. We sadly reflected, "We do a better job teaching our children the traditions of our alma maters than we do teaching them the faith." We echoed this mantra throughout seminary as we studied the faith formation of teenagers.

Our criticism was not directed at the parents of the teenagers we loved; we were examining our own practices, passions, and loyalties. These conversations were deeply rooted in lament. We lamented our own misguided priorities and the misguided priorities of the United States church around the faith development of teenagers. We love teenagers and we love God, and we desperately want teenagers to live into the fullness that is God's kingdom. As church leaders we want this for you, too! We desire to live more fully into this kingdom ourselves, and to serve God in youth ministry because we know that following Christ transforms people!

We lament the moments we miss great opportunities to teach the faith to young people in our families, churches, and communities. We lament the weaknesses in our own faith and our own faithlessness. We lament that we fail to share our passion for God's message and fail to live fully into the promised reality of God's kingdom on earth as it is in heaven. Since seminary, I mentally catch myself every time I sing the alma mater or babble endlessly about my college days. I ask myself, "Am I intentionally sharing my faith story with my own children, beyond what they hear from the pulpit on Sunday mornings?"

Even ordained pastors struggle to authentically share their faith with their teenagers. One pastor said, "My daughter thinks I read the Bible because it's my job." Some pastors wonder, "How do I teach my children the faith without them thinking it's just her job to read the Bible or pray?" As parents, maybe you think, "Isn't it the pastor's job to teach my family about God? Aren't we paying the youth pastor to teach our teens about Jesus?" The answer to all of these questions is yes, in some way. Yes, it is part of a pastor's job to read the Bible and pray. Yes, the pastor is responsible for explaining the faith, and yes, for those of you fortunate enough to have a youth pastor, it is the youth pastor's job to teach your young person about God. Even still, God gifted you and me with children and the responsibility (and joy) to teach them the faith. Isn't it life-giving to share hobbies, interests, and passions with your child? Didn't you love it when he or she fell in love with the activities you love? Remember the passion of the KSU dance reception rally—that little boy's family rejoiced in seeing their little guy articulate a love and passion for their school.

Think about why you intentionally taught your children basic life skills. Further, why have you exposed them to the arts, sports, or other interests? Why did you intentionally influence, guide, and cultivate their growth? Of the reasons that come to mind, one was likely because it was important—a priority. And despite having others around to help teach and coach, you felt you had a role to play—an incredibly important role. Consider that your teenager's

PARENT PRACTICE
As your teenager enters confirmation, how will you prioritize your teen's formation?

faith formation is an even higher priority and that your role in nurturing it is even more important.

Let's prioritize, shall we? As parents, we experience the pressures of setting our priorities based on the desires of teachers, coaches, and peers. Based on what the National Study of Youth and Religion research suggests, our priorities set the tone for the priorities of our teenager's faith. What great work might God do in and through you if you reprioritized your life and chose to start a spiritual practice such as beginning each day with ten minutes of silent prayer? What might happen if you began meeting with a group of friends for Bible study or asked God where you could use your gifts to serve your congregation and/or community?

Pat, a father of four girls, experienced God moving in his life in new ways. God sparked a desire for him to raise funds for the rescue mission in his local community. Pat invited friends and family to partner with him in living out God's mission in the world by providing food, clothing, and shelter to the disenfranchised in his community. Before websites promoted fundraising efforts, Pat e-mailed friends and family to invite them into God's work. At the end of the year, Pat reached his running goal and simultaneously fed the hungry, clothed the naked, and offered shelter to homeless people. Pat reordered his life by turning a simple daily exercise into a God-focused mission. This simple restructuring of a regular practice offered Pat a way to give God greater priority in his life. Years later, Pat is still running, blogging, and raising funds for various charities that carry out God's mission.

Sue set aside time every morning before her children woke up to sit in her chair, read the Bible, and write prayers in her prayer journal. Each morning as her high school daughter walked down the stairs to start her day, she witnessed her mother folding up her prayer journal, closing her Bible, and greeting her for the morning. Sue's children knew that spending time each day in the presence of God was a priority for their mother, they never had to ask if they were included in her prayers, and they saw the priority Sue placed on seeking God's presence in her life through her morning practices.

Priorities are difficult to talk about and challenging in today's culture, but the challenge of prioritizing our faith is not new. Jesus addressed priorities when he was walking the earth. One account that speaks to us on this is that of the rich young ruler in Mark 10:

> As Jesus continued down the road, a man ran up, knelt before him, and asked, "Good Teacher, what must I do to obtain eternal life?"
>
> Jesus replied, "Why do you call me good? No one is good except the one God. You know the commandments: *Don't commit murder. Don't commit adultery. Don't steal. Don't give false testimony.* Don't cheat. *Honor your father and mother.*"
>
> "Teacher," he responded, "I've kept all of these things since I was a boy."
>
> Jesus looked at him carefully and loved him. He said, "You are lacking one thing. Go, sell what you own, and give the money to the poor. Then you will have treasure in heaven. And come, follow me." But the man was dismayed at this statement and went away saddened, because he had many possessions.
>
> Looking around, Jesus said to his disciples, "It will be very hard for the wealthy to enter God's kingdom!" His words startled the disciples, so Jesus told them again, "Children, it's difficult to enter God's kingdom! It's easier for a camel to squeeze through the eye of a needle than for a rich person to enter God's kingdom."
>
> They were shocked even more and said to each other, "Then who can be saved?"

Jesus looked at them carefully and said, "It's impossible with human beings, but not with God. All things are possible for God."

Peter said to him, "Look, we've left everything and followed you."

Jesus said, "I assure you that anyone who has left house, brothers, sisters, mother, father, children, or farms because of me and because of the good news will receive one hundred times as much now in this life—houses, brothers, sisters, mothers, children, and farms (with harassment)—and in the coming age, eternal life. But many who are first will be last. And many who are last will be first."

(Mark 10:17-31)

Do you identify with the man's sadness in this story? Every single time I read this story, I find myself feeling sorry for the man whom Matthew and Luke identify as "rich" and a "young ruler." Then, I find myself getting defensive. I think, Surely Jesus isn't telling me to sell all of my worldly possessions. Why is Jesus so harsh toward the rich man? Jesus isn't fair—he's not fair at all! Why couldn't Jesus lighten the expectation just a little bit?

Inevitably, when we read this passage, it is hard not to be drawn to reread the part that says, "Jesus looked at him carefully and loved him." Jesus offers this man the absolute opportunity of a lifetime to go on an adventure that no amount of money could buy. Jesus sees the man and his worldly priorities and loves him! Amazing! Jesus invites the rich young ruler to be one of his disciples, to experience fullness of life, joy, an up-close and personal view of the miracles and teachings of Jesus, and the opportunity to shape the course of human history—and the man chooses his riches over this once-in-all-of-human-history opportunity.

It is sad to think that so many of us find ourselves identifying so closely with the rich young ruler. Time and time again,

Jesus invites us to let him set the agenda of our lives, and we walk away sad, because we want to keep our priorities and still receive the benefits of Jesus. We imagine that the reason the disciples sympathize with the man is that they did not realize how huge their opportunity was in being a disciple of Jesus until the end of their lives, or perhaps even in their deaths. At this moment, they may not have realized that the man's choice to follow his priorities instead of following Jesus would cost him much more than his riches. We find comfort in Jesus. He loves the man despite his choice to walk away from becoming a disciple.

Making our relationship with Christ the central priority comes at a high price, but in all fairness Jesus warned us. In Mark 8, Jesus told the disciples:

> Jesus said to them, "All who want to come after me must say no to themselves, take up their cross, and follow me. All who want to save their lives will lose them. But all who lose their lives because of me and because of the good news will save them. Why would people gain the whole world but lose their lives? What will people give in exchange for their lives?
> (Mark 8:34-37)

Jesus told the disciples that real life is experienced when our priorities reflect God's priorities. These passages are not intended to condemn us. Rather in God's goodness, and kindness, they beckon us into full, abundant life. A life centered upon Christ guarantees a life of promise, hope, and fulfillment! Jesus invited the rich young ruler to follow him on a life-altering journey. To follow Jesus, this man's daily priorities would have to be profoundly reordered.

The same invitation is offered to us. What opportunities do we miss when our lives are oriented around ourselves rather than around the purposes of God? Incorporating spiritual disciplines such as personal prayer, Bible study, worship, fasting, and service into our daily lives offers us ways to orient our lives around Christ and Christ's priorities in the world.

Worship Plus 2

Bishop Scott Jones encourages pastors and churches to be "Worship Plus 2" churches. I have gleaned from conversation with Bishop Jones this path to build our faith: he says that one way to increase our faith is to make worship attendance a top priority and then to connect with God in two other ways. Bishop Jones suggests the two other ways are finding a way to serve and finding a place to be served. What would Worship Plus 2 look like in your life? If Worship Plus 2 feels like too much, consider personal practices you might add to your daily or weekly routine. Create a gratitude journal, and every night before bed, list all of the things in life for which you are grateful. Choose one meal a week for fasting. During the weekly fast, take a walk and pray out loud to God for your family. As you start to incorporate spiritual disciplines into your life, increase your daily or weekly commitments over time by spending more time doing a spiritual discipline you enjoy or by adding new spiritual disciplines into your practices. Try it incrementally. In exercise, as you increase your strength and flexibility, you increase the amount of exercise. As with exercise, as you increase your spiritual strength and flexibility, increase your spiritual disciplines to match your growth.

Intentionally Intergenerational

In recent decades, many U.S. churches have created separate space on Sunday mornings for age-specific ministries while adults go to "big church." In some churches, a high school grad could attend a lifetime of age-specific worship without ever engaging the larger community of faith. In doing this, the church has unintentionally age-segregated the body of Christ, and in turn failed to teach children and teenagers how to participate in the greater Christian community. Teenagers suffer from this isolation, and adults suffer, too! Let's reverse this trend!

When young people participate in worship, they interact with an intergenerational community. Worshipping in an intergenerational faith community before graduation prepares them to find a church on their own and participate in the church after they graduate high school and go into the work force or head off to college. Intergenerational worship exposes teenagers to the wisdom of older generations, and increases their "great cloud of witnesses" with whom they can join in God's mission as full participants. If teenagers know how to act in worship only with their peers, it may be disorienting to be thrown into the strange land of intergenerational worship with all ages where the people surrounding them are not as much like them. Emerging adults who are accustomed to multi-age worship as children and teenagers tend to find themselves at home in an intergenerational worship service when they strike out on their own. In fact, the research from the Fuller Youth Institute says that the No. 1 factor linked to whether or not our children's faith will "stick" with them and develop into a mature faith in high school and college is their participation in intergenerational ministry.[12]

PARENT PRACTICE
Ask God to show you one habit you can add or delete from your life in order to give greater priority to your relationship with God. As a way of keeping yourself accountable to this habit, tell someone you trust your plan of action. Talk to your partner and agree on how you want to make worship a greater priority in your house. Determine how to discuss this with your family. Find a way to communicate your plan, and ask questions from your teenagers that will help create buy-in from them.

Let's Start Talking

What we say matters. One of the first steps we can take as parents to begin having deliberate faith conversations with our teens is to share stories about our faith experiences. It may feel awkward and uncomfortable at first, and that's OK! It's OK to start by saying, "I know we haven't talked much about my faith. I want tell you why my faith matters to me. I may sound awkward at times, but let's talk about it more, and the awkwardness will get better."

Teenagers often struggle to put words to their faith because they do not yet have a faith language. At first glance, you may think, "Well, that's not so abnormal. Putting words to faith can be difficult." Well, yes and no. Make a mental list of the ways your teenager is well-spoken. Teenagers' ability to articulate any number of topics is as wide as their interests, from art to football to movies, music, fashion, technology, politics, literature, robotics, and much more. Young people are smart. They have a vast array of knowledge. Teens have sophisticated conversations about many topics because someone taught them the language.

We cannot assume that teens will come to understand and live the Christian faith in the little time they spend in worship, Sunday school, or youth group. Think about the number of hours your teenager spends at musical rehearsal, soccer practice, piano lessons, and so forth. These skills are not learned over the course of one to two hours a week. Becoming a great pianist or all-star goalie takes both verbal instruction and repeated rehearsed action. The Christian faith is no different. It is learned and lived through word and deed. Jesus both taught with words about God's kingdom and led his disciples in putting those words into actions.

Beyond worship, Sunday school, and youth group, it is vital that followers of Jesus talk about our relationship with God with one another, especially adults with young people and specifically parents with their sons and daughters. Here's why. The National Study of Youth and Religion reveals that your religious practices and commitments are influential:

> Parents of teenagers appear to play an important role in the character of their children's religious lives. In the immediacy of parenting teenagers, parents may feel a loss of control and influence over their teens, but nationally representative statistics show that the religious practices and commitments of parents remain

an important influence on the religious practices and commitments of their teenage children.[13]

You may feel that faith is a private matter and try to avoid discussing topics of religion in general. While the good intention may be to keep peace and prevent harm, research shows that what we say and don't say about faith directly influences the faith formation of our children. Let's name the reality: starting a conversation about faith with your teenager can be very awkward. However, just like the stressful conversations most of us have with our emerging teenagers about subjects such as sex, it's well worth it to not leave them to figure it out on their own.

Storytelling is a simple yet powerful way to ease into the practice of sharing our faith with our teens. Our children love to know us better, and stories of our lives, choices, experiences, and learning give them new insight into who we are. Think of the family stories that were passed down to you and how they shaped you. Now consider a meaningful story from your teen years. Maybe you have one when you encountered God for the first time, said yes to following Jesus, or perhaps missed an opportunity to do something your faith told you to do. You may have not put your trust in Jesus until adulthood. You may be wrestling with your faith at this moment. By sharing our moments of faith—including our moments of doubt and failure—we create space for our teens to explore and experience God's mercy and compassion, to have the opportunity to embrace the story of Jesus as their own, and to embark on their own relationship with God. It might be uncomfortable at first, but the more you tell your stories, the more natural the conversations will become.

God is good, faithful, and trustworthy. God listens, loves, and provides for us in our parenting. God delights in loving us in the same way that we delight in our teenagers. May our trust in God increase as we seek to guide our teens into the way that leads to life eternal. God willingly, even eagerly, gives us the tools we need to nurture our children's faith. With God's grace and help, let's trust God for words to articulate our faith. Let's be deliberate in sharing with our teens about God's amazing work in our lives and in the world around us.

Let's Allow for Holy Interruptions

Moralistic Therapeutic Deism (MTD) was the most alarming aspect of the National Study of Youth and Religion. MTD is arguably the predominant religious perspective in the United States. When we adhere to MTD, we stop anticipating that God will surprise us with answered prayers; with places to step out in faith and trust God; and with unplanned opportunities to respond to God's invitation to be agents of justice and mercy in the world.

A person with a Moralistic Therapeutic Deism faith believes that:

1. God created the world and watches over human life.

2. God wants people to be good, nice, and fair to each other, as taught in the Bible and by most world religions.

3. The central goal of life is to be happy and to feel good about oneself.

4. God does not need to be involved in one's life except when problems arise.

5. Good people go to heaven when they die.[14]

> **PARENT PRACTICE**
> Don't know how to get started? Out of curiosity, ask your teenager some genuine questions. For example, you may say something like, "I'm really curious, what are your thoughts on the new Beyonce song? I've heard you singing it a lot. Why do you like it? I've been wondering all day how that song meshes with Pastor Cindy's sermon on forgiveness. What do you think?" Or say, "I know you've been feeling pressure from your friends. I'm praying for God's guidance to know what to do. How can I support you?"

You Matter Most 51

On the surface, none of the components of MTD appear to be bad. Who doesn't like a well-dressed, nice teenager with a healthy and overarching positive attitude that keeps them earning good grades, staying out of jail, and leading a happy life? The sometimes unintended consequence of MTD is that we look to God to endorse our choices and plans for our teenagers and ourselves rather than seek God for God's desires for us.

However, if we look more closely at the MTD tenets, we see where Christianity and MTD veer apart. Genesis 1 and 2 describe God as the Creator, and in these first chapters we see how God does far more than watch over human life. God nurtures creation, walks in the garden with Adam and Eve, and ensures that their every need is met. God invites Adam and Eve into far more than a life of being good, nice, and fair. God actually gives Adam and Eve stewardship and responsibility over creation. God grants them access to the entire garden except for one tree. Adam and Eve live in perfect harmony with God, each another, and creation. God created us to delight in the glory of God, and to participate in God's goodness. This offers a far deeper satisfaction than a healthy ego or circumstantial happiness. God offers us a life where we are restored to God's intention for us in creation before sin entered the scene. God designed us to live in full fellowship with God, one another, and the whole of creation. Full fellowship with God is an ongoing, consistent, steady relationship with God in good times and bad.

Finally, unlike MTD, in Christianity eternal life with Christ is not determined by our goodness or actions. Ephesians 2:8-10 states:

> You are saved by God's grace because of your faith. This salvation is God's gift. It's not something you possessed. It's not something you did that you can be proud of. Instead, we are God's accomplishment, created in Christ Jesus to do good things. God planned for these good things to be the way that we live our lives.

God created us to do good works with God, to be active in God's mission in the world, and to participate fully in God's kingdom. Living as Christians in the world means we open ourselves up to God rearranging our lives and our plans for God's purposes.

God interrupts our lives. Jesus' invitation to the rich young ruler was an interruption for the plans he made for his life. Interfering with our well-intended plans seems to be part of God's sanctifying grace at work. Through God's interruptions, God purges us of any impure motives that hinder our ability to faithfully serve God and care for others. This is the story found again and again in the biblical account. God unashamedly "wrecks" and "wastes" the life plans of many well-intentioned nice people in the Bible.

The disciples were doing their thing catching fish and keeping the family business lucrative until Jesus showed up. Can you imagine how the father of Simon and Andrew felt? After the father spent decades establishing the family business to pass down to his children, a man walks by and calls out, "Come, follow me, and I'll show you how to fish for people." Suddenly, in an unexpected moment, the father's whole life changes and the dreams he had for his boys are totally wrecked by a man named Jesus whose purposes and plans for his sons look nothing like he had imagined.

Or can you fathom being the mother of Mary? Can you imagine the mother being so close to having her daughter's future set, the dowry paid, the wedding preparations in order, the caterer hired, the reception planned, and the DIY decorations tucked away in every corner of the house? The mother worked so hard to arrange a future with a respectable man. She prepared her daughter to be self-sufficient, wise, and ready to be a strong life-partner to Joseph. Then, in one moment, all of the efforts, money, and relationship capital used to arrange a beautiful life for her daughter is totally wasted when the angel of the Lord shows up and persuades Mary to bear the Christ Child. This was not the happily ever after she envisioned for her baby girl!

God loves to interrupt our lives, and often God's interruptions seem anything but holy. God's interruptions feel impolite, abrupt, dangerous, and out of left field. Sometimes it takes years before we look back and realize that the unexpected twist on our path actually was God's holy interruption and that the holy interruption changed the trajectory of our lives forever in the most amazing way! Other times, we put out our own fleece to test God's holy interruption just to make sure we are hearing from God correctly.

Many times it is in hindsight that we see the joy, hope, and profound peace of God we experienced through responding to the disorienting movement of God in our lives. For Simon, Andrew, Mary, and us, the rewards in recognizing and responding to the upheaval of God's invitation cannot be measured in monetary value, power, prestige, or popularity.

When we offer our young people a life hidden in Christ that is expectant of holy interruptions rather than an MTD life, we offer them the assurance that God will guide their steps and hear the cries of their hearts. It doesn't assure us that God's calling for our children will match our hopes, dreams, and desires for them. Remember parents Jack and Teresa, whose faithful discipleship was described at the beginning of this chapter? God's calling took one of their daughters to Honduras, when that country was served by the Peace Corps, and another daughter across the country to podiatry school.

Sharing the Christian life with our teenagers not only means that we tell them the importance of trusting God with their lives and of listening to God's call, but it also requires that we trust God with our teenagers' lives. Giving our time, talents, treasures, gifts, and children to God guarantees us the opportunity to be a part of something far larger than ourselves and to make a positive difference in the world. Participating in daily life with Christ with our teens gives us the chance to participate together in God's mission of bringing hope to hopeless people, light to the dark places, and joy in areas of sorrow. Imagine what a positive force our children will be if we instill in them today a sense of possibility in following Christ.

Jessica loved going to the housing projects with her youth group. Every week Jessica tore into the church parking lot ready to tutor children in the neighborhood adjacent to her local church. She never missed serving in the after-school program. Jessica latched on to the most difficult children in the program. She offered them unconditional love and educational tools to help them succeed in school. Jessica dreamed of becoming a high school math teacher in her hometown until God wrecked her plans.

Her weekly visits to the projects opened the door for God to disorient Jessica's future. As a high school junior and senior, Jessica found ways to serve beyond the youth director's weekly plans. Jessica drove herself to the projects and designed her own ministry to the children by organizing a Christmas party complete with personal Christmas packages for each child.

By the time Jessica graduated from high school, she was completely captivated with God's mission for educating children in poverty. After college, she returned to her hometown in Florida to serve a low-income elementary school. Later, she earned a graduate degree focused on child advocacy in the public school setting. Now, she teaches elementary students in an inner city in South Carolina.

Jessica's parents, Rob and Tina, understood that Jessica's faith in God hinged on their faith in God, and they trusted God through these holy disruptions. Like Jack and Teresa, Rob and Tina trust God with their children. These couples know the difficulty and challenge of entrusting their children to God's care. The journey has brought both excitement and struggle for both sets of parents. Yet their trust in God's leading and responsiveness to holy interruptions in their teens' lives have resulted in a deeper faith for their families.

How might God's holy interruptions in the lives of your teenager also draw you into deeper fellowship with God?

PARENT PRACTICE
Every morning this week, set aside ten minutes to sit in silence. Turn off the radio in your car, wake up earlier and grab a cup of coffee, or turn off your electronics before bed. Wherever you find this place of solace, take a deep breath and invite God to open your eyes to the holy interruptions before you.

Really, You Matter the Most!

Are you convinced yet? Your influence is more powerful than the influence of anyone else in your teen's life. Mom, I know it's hard to believe that your Instagram drama-driven, Axe deodorant-covered 13-going-on-30-year-old son is paying attention. Dad, would you ever believe your "Daddy, please don't embarrass me" 14-year-old baby girl listens to what you say about God more than she listens to her pastor, her Sunday school teacher, her youth director, or even her "oh so cool" college intern? (It's hard for the intern to believe, too!) But facts are facts! Parents, despite whatever insecurities, doubts, questions, and internal battles you face about raising your teenager as a person of faith, no one is more significant in your teen's faith development than you. So now that you know the facts—before you get too scared, close the book, and run—remember God's promise in James 1:5:

> But anyone who needs wisdom should ask God, whose very nature is to give to everyone without a second thought, without keeping score. Wisdom will certainly be given to those who ask.

God equips us with the Holy Spirit to guide, comfort, teach, and lead us in all things, including parenting. Ask God for wisdom, seek God for wisdom, listen for God's wisdom, and know God gives wisdom generously! It is God's very nature to give wisdom to those seeking wisdom. The teenagers we love so much loves us and trusts us the most when it comes to matters of the heart. Our teenagers need us to recognize and respond to God's presence and need us to teach them how to recognize and respond to God's presence.

Chapter 3 Notes

1. Christian Smith with Melinda Lundquist Denton, *Soul Searching: The Religious and Spiritual Lives of American Teenagers* (New York: Oxford University Press, 2005), page 57.
2. Smith, *Soul Searching*, page 57.
3. Smith, *Soul Searching*, page 261.
4. Smith, *Soul Searching*, page 91.
5. Smith, *Soul Searching*, page 120.
6. Smith, *Soul Searching*, page 261.
7. Smith, *Soul Searching*, page 260.
8. Kenda Creasy Dean, *Almost Christian: What the Faith of Our Teenagers Is Telling the American Church* (New York: Oxford University Press, 2010), page 204.
9. Smith, *Soul Searching*, page 260.
10. Smith, *Soul Searching*, pages 261-262.
11. Smith, *Soul Searching*, pages 162-163.
12. Kara Powell, Brad Griffin, and Cheryl Crawford, "The Church Sticking Together," 17 October 2011, StickyFaith.org, tinyurl.com/3cnqclu, accessed 10 August 2016, as adapted from Kara Powell, Brad Griffin, and Cheryl Crawford, "Sticky Churches," chapter 4 in *Sticky Faith, Youth Worker Edition* (Grand Rapids: Zondervan, 2011), pages 71-95.
13. Smith, *Soul Searching*, pages 115-116.
14. Smith, *Soul Searching*, pages 162-163.

4 Activities for Home

Now that we know what the research says about our role in forming the faith of our teens, how do we put our knowledge into action? This final chapter offers practical ways for you to engage your family in intentional faith conversations and activities. Experiment and find out what works best for you and your teenager.

Car Convos

As parents, we spend hours in the car shuttling our children to and from school, practices, friends' houses, camps, and a myriad of other activities. These car rides can be times of heightened stress as we battle traffic to make it on time, or they can be needed pauses in the midst of varying degrees of chaos. Imagine transforming regular, humdrum car rides to church, soccer practice, or piano lessons into conversations about faith. With a simple discussion starter in the car, you can create the opportunity for deeper conversation during the drive or later over ice cream or dinner.

Car Convos—or car conversations—offer creative ways for you to talk to your confirmand about God at a time when your teen is most available and receptive. The following suggestions provide instructions for how to create experiences in the car for your family to draw closer to God and one another by talking about God, specifically as your teen enters the confirmation process. These are practices you could establish at the onset of confirmation, and expand upon once your teen more fully grasps his or her own faith. These practices give you ways to enter into the learning occurring in the confirmation classroom and offer you ways to develop habits for faith formation to last long after confirmation ends.

Here are some recommendations as you start to establish a pattern for regular Car Convos:

- Explain to your teen that that you'd like to use a regular car ride each week to bring up two questions about confirmation that you can discuss together.

- Think about your teen's mood throughout the week and suggest a regular car ride that allows ample time for conversation. Pick a time in the week when your teen is more apt to talk, or ask your teen to help you determine the best time for a Car Convo.

- Ask your teen, "Which do you prefer—either discussing the same two topics each week throughout all of confirmation or mixing it up with a variety of questions?" Give a reminder so the teen can be thinking about the questions in advance.

- These Car Convos might start with the simple question, "How did you experience God this week in confirmation?" Another question to get started is something like, "What did you learn about yourself this week?" (For more potential questions for your Car Convos, consider the list of questions later in the chapter.)

TIP
Consider the personality of your teen. Does she or he prefer being spontaneous with questions or being prepared with the same questions each week? Your teen's preferences may be different from your own, so go the teen's direction for success. Why not even involve your teen in this part of the discussion? Maybe say, "I want to stay connected throughout confirmation so I know what you are learning, and you can give me insight into what God is doing within you. How could we do that?"

Activities for Home

59

Dinner Devos

If Car Convos might not work for you, you can give Dinner Devos a try. Research has told us for decades how important it is for families to eat dinner together. One family I know credited evening meals through tough years as the glue that kept their family together. Later in life, the children shared that they attributed their parents' long-lasting marriage to regular family dinners. The dinner table fostered space for everyone to come together and work through the good and bad moments of life. Meaningful conversation with your family on major questions of faith around the dinner table not only provides your family the joy of spending time together but also turns the dinner table into a sacred place for shaping young disciples and building a family legacy. If this sounds a lot like what Jesus did with his disciples, it should. Through something as simple as dinner devotionals, you can demonstrate the value of confirmation to your confirmand and your other children by openly guiding and learning from and with your teen around the dinner table.

In case you haven't guessed, one of the greatest benefits to the Dinner Devo is the opportunity to incorporate the entire family in the confirmation process. Whether you decide to share stories of your faith journey or talk about a particular confirmation lesson, you are encouraging and leading your family to trust Jesus in a fun and engaging way. The hardest part about this is, of course, getting started. Let confirmation be the spark, and take advantage of the opportunity for this to become a sacred time and place for deepening your family's faith.

Here are some suggestions for getting started on Dinner Devos:

- First, pick a night or a few nights of the week when you will have your devos.

- As with Car Convos, Dinner Devos may start with the two simple questions such as, "Where did you experience God this week?" or "What did you learn about yourself through confirmation?"

TIPS

If you have an incredibly introspective teen, do consider having the questions available ahead of time so that he or she is prepared to discuss the questions at dinner.

Use questions that best fit your teen's interests. Think about what you hear your teen saying and use questions that match the teen best, or include him or her in the process of choosing the questions.

Consider giving the twelve questions to your teen and letting the teen choose the questions that he or she will answer for the week. Or for the more adventurous, print and cut the questions into paper strips and have your teen draw one out of a jar. And how about supplying some blank paper strips to write questions on or to put into the jar blank for a "free," teen-chosen topic?

- Give everyone in the family the opportunity to answer these questions. (You may have to adjust the questions for younger children.)

- You might also consider making a list of questions on note cards and placing the note cards on your dinner table. Then take turns letting different family members choose the question for the week.

- Depending on how much your family enjoys spontaneity, choose the question randomly as dinner begins. If your family prefers to have time to think about their responses, designate one family member to pick the question in advance and share. (The following list of questions may help you determine the questions to use in Dinner Devos.)

Twelve Questions

1. What was a lightbulb moment for you this week?

2. What is one characteristic of God you discovered today?

3. Share one concept or idea that challenged your thinking this week.

Activities for Home

4. What is one thing you would like to do based on what you learned?

5. What stumped you?

6. Describe a doubt that you experienced from this week's lesson.

7. How did you experience God in this week's lesson?

TIP
Sometimes an indirect way to get to your own teen's thoughts or feelings is to ask about their friends' thoughts or feelings.

8. Rate this week's lesson on a scale of 1 to 10, with 10 being excellent. If your teen chooses an 8, ask, "What kept it from being a 9 or why didn't you rate it a 7?"

9. How did you connect with the lesson this week?

10. What did you love about this week's topic? What did you hate about it?

11. What do you agree with in the lesson? What do you question in the lesson?

12. What did your friends like about this week's lesson? What did they dislike?

Parent Initiated Activities

The following activities are for you to initiate with your teenager during confirmation. You are the one to prep and design. You will work together with your teen to complete them.

1. Design a family tree that tells the history of your family's faith. Did you have any pastors or missionaries in your family tree? What denominations are represented? Do you have a long line of United Methodists? What special stories of faith have you heard over many generations? Do you have any family

traditions around faith? Share the faith tree with your teen during confirmation or give it to them as a confirmation gift.

2. Select other faith communities to attend with your family. Avoid services that overlap your teen's confirmation class. Consider attending a Roman Catholic Mass, finding a nondenominational worship service, or going to a Jewish synagogue. Ask your family to list similarities and differences between your faith community and the faith community you experienced together. Encourage conversations about what they liked or disliked about the other faith communities.

3. Set aside an hour to remember your child's baptism. Invite family and friends who were present at your child's baptism to join you, or send messages about that day. Tell stories of the infant baptism, show pictures, and write a letter to your teen with the details you remember from their baptism. Your pastor has a formal liturgy for remembering a baptism in *The United Methodist Book of Worship,* so consider asking your pastor to create a way to help your family and friends remember your child's baptism. This could be a surprise or something you plan with your teen.

4. Fill a prayer journal with prayers for your teen. At the start of confirmation, buy a blank journal, and over the course of confirmation, write your prayers for your teenager in the journal. After confirmation, give the journal to your confirmand as a gift.

5. Visit a nature center, take a hike, go fishing, or take a long bike ride together. Leave electronics at home and spend this time together. Before you go, encourage everyone to look out for God sightings. On the way home, invite everyone to share how God was experienced during your unplugged time together; use words, draw pictures, or do both.

6. Search for family-friendly service opportunities in your area. Invite your teenager to make the final decision from a short list, and spend one afternoon or evening serving together.

7. Find a devotional and read it together daily or weekly. Your pastor or confirmation teacher can help you find a good devotional for this purpose.

8. Start a family evening prayer routine Simply list three things each that you're grateful for, and then recite the Lord's Prayer together. As your comfort level increases, consider spontaneously praying aloud.

9. Memorize a passage of Scripture together. Psalm 23 is a good starting place. Or have your teen choose a passage.

10. Pick a book of the Bible to read as a family. Perhaps as part of your Dinner Devos, you could read a chapter together once a week or have everyone read a chapter and come ready for family discussion. Start with three simple questions for discussion:

- What was interesting to you?
- What questions do you have?
- Where do you see God in this passage?

Conclusion

This parent guide is not a comprehensive "how to parent your teenager through confirmation." Our desire is that it would be a tool that helps you better understand your role in confirmation, your influence in the faith formation of your teenager, and a way to gain confidence in giving guidance to your teen. We pray that you feel encouraged and renewed in your own faith as well as more equipped for that sacred responsibility.